The Cherrywood Challenge 2014: WICKED

Published by
Cherrywood Hand Dyed Fabrics, Inc.

Concept and Design by Karla Overland
Photography by John Overland

ISBN: 978-0-9863417-0-0

Cherrywood Hand Dyed Fabrics, Inc.
P.O. Box 486
Brainerd, Minnesota 56401
888-298-0967
www.cherrywoodfabrics.com

Are you wicked? What does "wicked" mean to you?

The idea for The WICKED Cherrywood Challenge was born while planning a trip to New York City to see the musical production. Inspired by the spectacular set, amazing costumes, and meaningful story of *WICKED*, Karla Overland (owner of Cherrywood) developed the parameters for the first Cherrywood Challenge. The idea was pitched to the producers of *WICKED* who embraced it, agreeing to display the finalists in the Gershwin Theater in New York City as an added incentive. The quilts hung on Broadway for two months, drawing attention and surprise at the non-traditional nature of the quilts.

THE **WICKED**™ **CHERRYWOOD CHALLENGE** 2014

A quilt challenge sponsored by Cherrywood Hand Dyed Fabrics

ARE YOU WICKED?

www.cherrywoodfabrics.com

In early 2014, an open invitation was announced for quilters and fiber artists to submit a 20"x 20" quilt using any techniques they chose. Quilts had to be made entirely from Cherrywood Fabric, primarily using Onyx and the three Wicked Greens dyed exclusively for this challenge. As the August 1st deadline approached and the entries rolled in, it became obvious the theme was a hit. *The Q Gallery* in Brainerd, Minnesota, provided the perfect setting to display all the entries - an unexpected 114!

The Q Gallery, Franklin Art Center, Brainerd, Minnesota

When the spotlights switched on, it was absolutely breathtaking! It was exactly what Karla envisioned - a cohesive collection of artwork held together by a flood of gorgeous lime green and black Cherrywood. The strong visual impact of this exhibit was due not only to the limited color palette, consistent size, and interesting theme, but also to the amount of thought and detail each artist put into the quilts. Five judges representing a diversity of viewpoints had the challenging task of narrowing the entries to 27 Finalists, including Grand Prize, First Place, and Second Place.

The Q Gallery, Franklin Art Center, Brainerd, Minnesota

Whether inspired by the Broadway hit musical or all the wicked ways of the world, the images in these quilts are wickedly inspirational.

Spotlight

Lynn Synhorst
Fargo, North Dakota

Since I saw the play in New York, I thought this challenge would be very fun. One of the most exciting parts is the lights and how they reflect. The use of circles and the cogs as geometric shapes gives *WICKED* a modern look. I used scrapbook punches to create the shimmer of lights or stars that really bring the sparkle to Broadway. Takes you to the land of Oz!

Sandi Snow
Lutz, Florida

Time To Be Wicked is designed to be a visual synopsis of the musical. The pieced green background represents the challenges of being green. Elphaba is boxed in by three black borders of dark tricks and mean-spirited jokes. One side provides an opening for Elphaba to follow her heart as she looks for good. The clock shows time changing jealousy and hatred to a true friendship between Elphaba and Glinda.

Time to Be Wicked

SECOND PLACE

Madame Morrible's Garden of Hexes, Poisons, and Potions

Robin Gausebeck
Rockford, Illinois

Madame Morrible's Garden is a WICKED perversion of the traditional grandmother's flower garden quilt pattern, populated by hexagonal flowers. It is a seemingly innocuous place but who knows what lies hidden among the forbidding-looking trees and poisonous-looking plants? The garden is watched over and guarded by a fearsome flying monkey perched on a desiccated branch and the yellow brick winding path leads to ... where? Only a personage as wicked as Madame Morrible would enjoy a leisurely stroll through this garden.

A brief summary of the musical *WICKED*

WICKED tells the incredible, previously untold story of an unlikely but profound friendship between two girls who first meet as sorcery students at Shiz University: the blonde and very popular Glinda and a misunderstood green girl named Elphaba.

Elphaba has a knack for magic, so the headmistress Madame Morrible sends her and Glinda to the Emerald City to help The Wonderful Wizard of Oz. However, The Wizard is not so wonderful and is segregating the talking animals in Oz from the rest of society. Elphaba is enraged, as she identifies with the outcast animals.

The girls' friendship reaches a crossroad, and their lives take very different paths. Elphaba's determination to remain true to herself and to those around her, has unexpected, shocking consequences for her future: she is tricked into creating the flying monkeys, forcing her to fulfill her destiny as Wicked Witch of the West. No matter how hard she tries to be "good," the propoganda from The Wizard forever labels her as "wicked." Glinda's unflinching desire for popularity sees her seduced by power. She remains "good" because she doesn't have the courage to defy The Wizard. Instead of standing up for her green friend, Glinda spins the rumors in her favor. She embraces the title of Glinda the Good.

In the end, The Wicked Witch isn't actually melted ... she escapes to live a secret life with her true love. Glinda has been affected by all the tragedy and becomes a better, less shallow person.

The musical pays homage to the classic *Wizard of Oz* story while simultaneously changing fans' understanding of it forever.

A cautionary tale about love, friendship, and trust, *WICKED* effortlessly reveals there are indeed two sides to every story.

Stephanie Adams

Kansas City, Kansas

Wicked Beauty

When I created this piece I wanted to make Elphaba the main focal point.
I decided to place her within the Dragon Clock where some say she came from.
I chose shades of vivid greens that represented Elphaba throughout the quilt. For the quilting,
I did swirls that mimicked the wicked winds of a tornado.

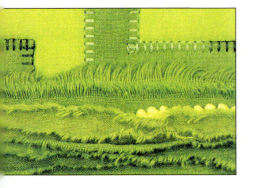

Judith Allen

Battle Creek, Michigan

Friends & Family

A story of two young women and their struggle to survive the impact of friends, family, and the world they live in.

Nicki Allen
Springfield, Virginia

Broadway Beauty

I love *WICKED!* I was fortunate to see *WICKED* at the Gershwin Theater in August 2013. When I learned about Cherrywood's WICKED Challenge, I immediately knew that part of my quilt would contain a New York beauty block. Inspired by Victoria Findlay Wolfe's method of constructing quilts, the rest of the quilt took shape literally in bits and pieces, as I "made" the fabric for the borders. I added in red because not only does it symbolize my affection for this fabulous show and the city in which I saw it, it also is the perfect complement to the beautifully WICKED greens.

FINALIST

Ellen Ault
Tampa, Florida

Monkey Wrench

This quilt was definitely out of my comfort zone. I never work with these type of colors. I added the purple binding to give a little 'pop'. I wanted to create a simple, graphic design with the gears and whimsy with the flying monkey. I loved the gradations of the greens and tried to add depth with them and the stitching. I didn't want to over-quilt it. You should focus on the monkey!

Rhonda Baldwin
Grand Island, Nebraska

Let Them Be

Leaves of three, let them be… a WICKED spell indeed. Anyone who has been affected by poison ivy knows how devious the little plant can be. Seemingly so pretty in a chartreuse gown, hiding among the weeds but actually waiting there to spring out and dust you with her WICKED poison. Free-hand cut and fused. Free-motion quilting.

Michelle Banton
Lunenburg, Massachusetts

Wonderfully Wicked in Oz

Growing up in Kansas, I was always familiar with The Wizard of Oz. This challenge let me play with beautiful fabric and learn the pre-story of Oz. I quilted bubbles because of Galinda. I learned the ruby slippers were originally silver. And I love the "steam punk" look of the musical's sets so I tried to incorporate that with the gears and clocks.

Erica Baron
Kingston, New York

Defying Gravity

This was my favorite moment in the show, Elphaba singing "Defying Gravity". The other elements in the quilt are taken from other visual details of the show: the clock face with 13 hours, the flying monkeys, and the border of the map of Oz. The quilt is hand appliquéd and machine pieced, quilted by hand and machine, and includes machine thread painting.

Susan Barten
Nelson, Minnesota

Wicked Leaves
A pop of red is all you see. Leaves change, good or bad, life goes on, never perfect.

Peggy Bass
Holton, Kansas

Embrace Your Inner Witch
I wanted this simple so the fabric colors were the focal ingredient.

Mel Beach
San Jose, California

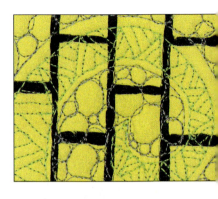

Wicked Windy & Winding Ways

This quilt symbolizes the interconnected paths of the characters from the musical. The fused center depicts the yellow brick road that connects Munchkinland to Emerald City. Two spirals wind their way out from the center: one quilted with bubbles that carry the ever bubbly Galinda, and the second spiral stitched in a green maze of triangles and crosshatching, reminiscent of Elphaba and her broom and witch hat. The large ticker tape tornado and mini twisters quilted along the border signify the windy transport of Dorothy and other characters to the great land of Oz.

FINALIST

Anna Berger
Santa Clara, California

Bad, Evil, Wicked
I love to work off the wonderful gradations of Cherrywood Fabrics!
This gave me the idea to use color to represent the three levels of badness
with the brightest and most acid green representing *WICKED*!

Wendy Blanton
Cumming, Georgia

Transformation

Merriam-Webster says *Transformation* represents a complete or major change. The forest is dying out, the monkeys are now flying and Elphaba has gone through many major changes during her short life. This Cherrywood Challenge has gone through many changes from design, to stitching and techniques. Creating this challenge was a constant learning process with many trials and errors. I discharged some black fabric to create rocks, used Angelina to make Oz shine, and Prismacolor pencils to add color to the monkeys.

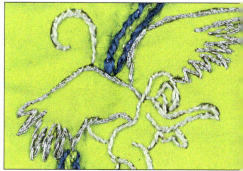

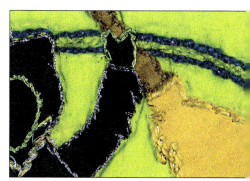

Audrey Bragstad
Pequot Lakes, Minnesota

Elphaba Thropp

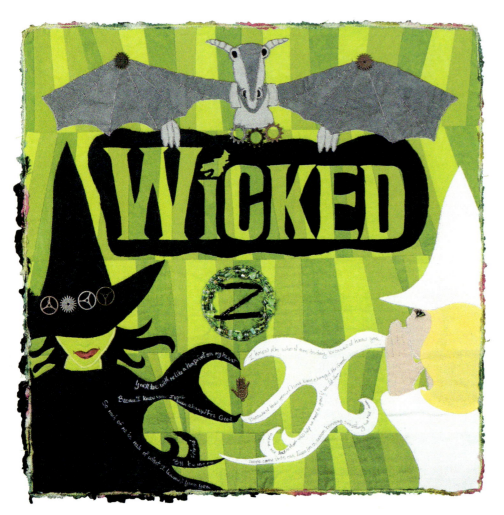

Deborah Bright
Fort Worth, Texas

For Good

This project spoke to my heart because I am a fan of musicals and have seen *WICKED* multiple times. We all change each other as we interact. Music and art should always walk hand-in-hand.

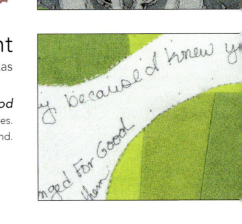

Phyllis Campbell
Rockford, Illinois

Witchy Woman

Rows of light and dark green, with chevrons in brighter green, form the background of my quilt. The woman, or female, symbol and the curvy appliquéd "W" represent the WICKED Challenge theme, with a small curved witch hat on the center moon-like circle. Quilted with a variegated thread and finished with a black binding, my *Witchy Woman* quilt makes a bold yet feminine WICKED statement for this fun challenge.

Enjoy!
Phyllis Campbell

Laurie Ceesay
Menominee, Michigan

Wicked Commotion

I love witches and green skin so this challenge was for me! I captured a whimsical Elphaba with her dress that appears black until viewed close up. I embellished with net trim, metallic trim, beaded lace, shimmery ribbon and beads to give color and texture to Elphaba's dress. I love to quote "I don't cause commotions, I am one" and added a version of the quote in lettering. I embellished the hat with fabric paint, a leather button and metallic trim. Elphaba's face has added fabric paint and nail polish for bling to bring her to life!

Stephanie Chandler
Chickamauga, Georgia

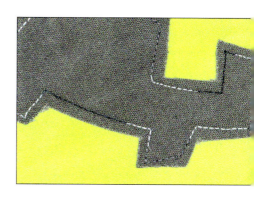

Heart Drop

The loss of a loved one, whether they love another or go away, can change a person forever. While the witch looks upon the land, her heart falls out of her chest, leaving a sad lonely person - creating a space for evil to grow.

Elaine Chapman
Sarasota, Florida

Chistery

Chistery became a flying monkey when the Wizard, who was trying to do away with the intelligent animals that lived in Oz, conned Elphaba into casting a spell from the Grimmerie, an ancient book of spells. Instead of the intended spell, Chistery and all the other monkeys painfully grew wings. The Wizard was actually trying to use Elphaba's powers to create spies and enemies for the Ozians. In more modern times, a "flying monkey" or "winged monkey" is known in the psychological world as being an enabler for a narcissist, who torments the intended victim in various ways.

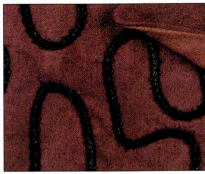

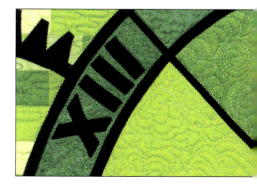

Marguerite Crum
West Lafayette, Indiana

Wicked Takes NY

We saw *WICKED* on Broadway in 2011 when we were in town for the Westminster dog show (so there's a quilted paw print). We loved it and I'm delighted to have this opportunity to honor it in the quilt. Since *WICKED* is an integral part of NYC, Elphaba and the palace are part of the new skyline. There are quilted "twin ghost towers" because that was "a whole 'nother kind of WICKED." This quilt is hand appliquéd, hand and machine pieced, machine embroidered and machine quilted. It also contains acrylic paint and crystals.

Michael Cunningham
Kingwood, Texas

Everyone Deserves the Chance to Fly

I am a self-taught artist who creates because I am driven to do so; my work is largely intuitive. Creativity has always been a part of my life; creativity equals growth. My aspirations are simple: to create fiber art/art quilts (a medium I am passionate about) and to share them with the public. Currently I work in thickened dyes and the limitless possibilities of how they can change the color but not the hand of the fabric. I strive to listen to the work and allow it to reveal itself; it is my practice to have many conversations going simultaneously.

Catherine Cureton
Cedar Park, Texas

One Short Day
I used the contrast of the green and black Cherrywood Hand Dyed Fabrics to capture Elphaba's iconic pose from the *WICKED* poster as she stands in front of the clock of the Time Dragon. She is ready to enter the Emerald City. Longarm quilting, hand embroidery, and fabric paints are used to add additional texture, depth, and color.

Roberta DeLuz
Benicia, California

Patchwork Wing
I didn't want a traditional flying monkey so I went with patchwork wings to be attached to the monkey. The face is a combination of thread painting and fabric markers.

Nancy Downey
Belgrade Lakes, Maine

Hats Off to "WICKED" (Eleven Years and Running)

As an inveterate homebody and firm believer in the powers of a great pair of shoes, I have long been a fan of *Wizard of Oz*, so I was thrilled to have the opportunity to pay tribute to *WICKED*. Raw-edge appliqué proved to be the best technique for the ragged, creepy vibe I wanted to achieve. Freely hand-quilting the brooms was a great reprieve after years of trying to achieve perfectly even, tiny quilting stitches

Pat DuBois
Woodbury, Minnesota

It's All About "The Tornado"

I have always loved *The Wizard of Oz*. Although I have never seen *WICKED* I really enjoyed the book and the whole idea of looking back into the life of the Wicked Witch. I knew right away I wanted a tornado for my challenge. Whether you call it a tornado, a cyclone, or a twister … it's the most powerful and WICKED of all. I had fun adding the other elements. I used paper piecing, curved piecing, needle turn appliqué, fusing, embroidery and even stepped outside my box and used crystals.

Olivia Duer Nelson
Navarre, Florida

Poor Elphaba

Brilliant, idealistic and - in her own way - lovely, Elphaba rages against the disappointment, bitterness and pain that plague her life, like a knife plunged into the heart and twisted ... over and over again.

Pam Duffy
Mead, Oklahoma

Which Way to Oz
Paper pieced with Judy Niemeyer papers. Pieced and quilted by Pam Duffy.

FINALIST

Kathy Durochik
Wheaton, Illinois

Wicked - Deconstructed

Deconstructed text has always been intriguing to me. I use the iconic logo from the play *WICKED* to design the main body of the quilt. It was cut up and rearranged. I choose to use the theater marquee lights as a border. A copy of the original design is on the back of the quilt. How very WICKED to slice up something that took hours to create!

Nancy Eisenhauer
Belleville, Illinois

The Source

Representing a concrete object is easy. Representing a concept is not. What better symbol of wickedness than an apple? Those familiar with the story from Genesis will immediately make the connection. The addition of the hand offering the forbidden fruit and the tempting serpent fill out the story as a visual image. I try to offer images from which viewers can create meaning.

Pam Evans
Shorewood, Minnesota

Wicked

I've been a stepmom for 20 years to two lovely young women, now 25 and 23. I would cheer for the stepmoms in Disney movies. For fun, my daughters would buy me "villain" Disney items. I loved seeing *WICKED* in the theater, and have always loved The Wizard of Oz – so my mission was to incorporate the two into one piece. I think I succeeded in doing that!

Paula Fleischer
Valencia, California

Elphaba's Ride

Pentagonal crazy-quilt blocks with dense hand embroidery and beading represent the costumes and set of Oz residents in *WICKED*. Elphaba's comment to Glinda about their differing mode of transportation is embroidered across the top. There are small black gears and metallic spirals to evoke the steam punk aesthetic. Just like *WICKED*, it takes a few viewings to see all of the details!

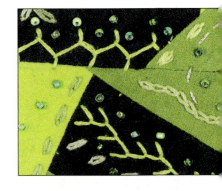

Stephanie Forsyth
Eden Prairie, Minnesota

Oz: The Redlight District

When trying to decide my direction for this challenge, I saw a girl with a pinup girl tattoo and thought it was exquisitely WICKED. What better kind of WICKED than a pinup girl with feather boas! The quilting is a combination of feathers and McTavishing.

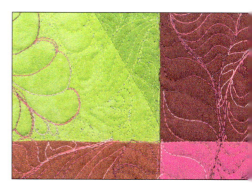

Marilyn Fromherz
Calimesa, California

B-Witched and B-Jeweled

Inspired by the musical, I created elements that peaked my interest. Elphaba needed a new hat and it is featured with a beautiful pink flower gift from Glinda to help her become "popular". Colorful monkey wings, a magic wand, a witch's broom, a clock, and gears are all creatively combined with beads and jewels to illustrate my WICKED art. The background is pieced blocks of green with digitally printed music and machine quilted with a fun web.

Lisa Gandre
West Allis, Wisconsin

Wicked Dress
Quilt Couture is a combination of quilt, garment and upholstery techniques blended to create unique pieces to view, wear and enjoy! *Wicked Dress* showcases garment making details - appliquéd dress, draped skirt, ruffle at the shoulder, shaped cuff and peplum and Swarovski crystals throughout.

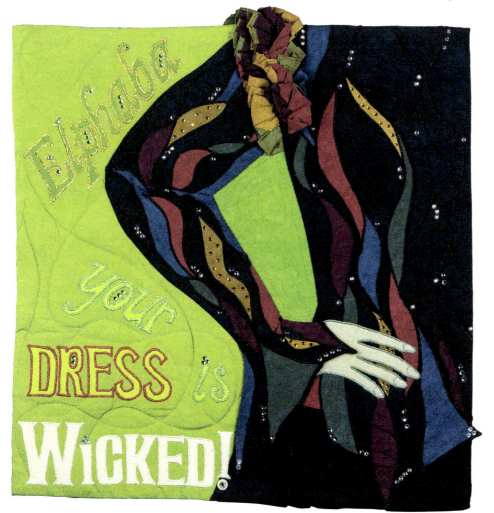

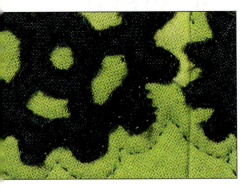

Lisa Giesfeldt
Sussex, Wisconsin

Wicked Comes to Wisconsin
Playing on the theme, five shades of green, from light to darkest, have been pieced into 100 two-inch blocks to represent two styles of monkey wrench blocks, surrounded by twister blocks. Elphaba's hats surround the central clock. Each corner has the ever-present cogs and gears.

FINALIST

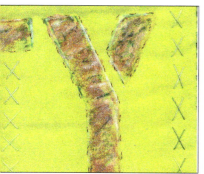

Sandi Goldman
Annandale, Virginia

Defy Gravity
Don't let your troubles weigh you down; be the best you can be;
do what you were meant to do; make the world a better place.

Lesly-Claire Greenberg

Fairfax, Virginia

Wicked Thorns

I am totally obsessed with the thorn. My continuing series of thorn quilts are all done with Cherrywood Fabrics - another one of my obsessions. Over the years I have collected yardage of every Cherrywood acid green. Though I haven't seen the play, I did read the book. For me this was a no-brainer - I was compelled to participate. I think there may be more WICKED quilts that need making.

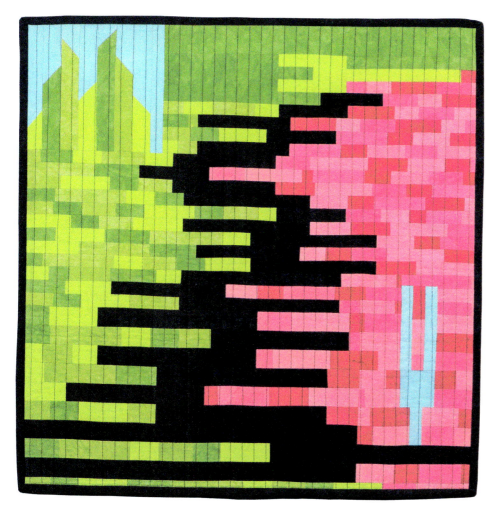

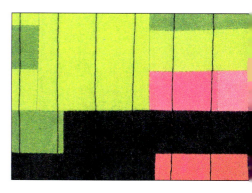

Kathy Greer
Port Angeles, Washington

Wickedly Tuned

To reflect WICKED as a modern musical, I chose to work with tuning forks and color. Elphaba and Glinda are represented as tuning forks, with Elphaba's modified to look broom-like, flying away from Oz. The stacked black tuning forks in the center are intended to give the impression of a witch's hat and capture the divide in Elphaba and Glinda's relationship. The multi-hued green and pink backgrounds are intended to reflect stage lighting.

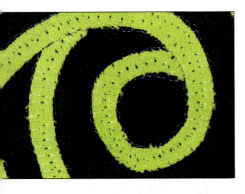

Becky Grover
Ann Arbor, Michigan

Changing Paths
What do you do when the path you start out on was no longer the right one? Or when it shifts? There are so many possible paths out there. How do you choose?

piece everyday
Karen Grover

Karen Grover
Rockford, Illinois

Oh No!

Meet Esme, witch-in-training. She really needs practice making flying monkeys.
She has been practicing, diligently, kind of. Practice does eventually get boring.
With an impishly WICKED look, she swishes her wand and creates a blizzard (oh no),
a catbird (oh no), and a bockadoodle-doo! Oh no!

Jane Hall

Raleigh, North Carolina

Pineapples for Elphaba

I work most often with the pieced pineapple block, and this variation is a favorite. It is a hybrid pineapple and log cabin design where the opposing corners produce completely different graphics: one set is a traditional pineapple "star", while the other forms log cabin "balls of color". Given the colors in the challenge, I could immediately see multi-shades of green spheres against black. There are several dye lots of blacks, as well as a dark purple, which help create an interesting textured background for Elphaba's greens. Pieced on a foundation by machine.

FINALIST

Cena Harmon
Pensacola, Florida

Envy

"I long to be popular, rich, pretty and thin.
Oh, the green-eyed monster lurks deep within."
Our WICKED nature may be revealed when desires turn to envy.

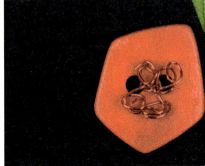

Dawn Hebert
Fargo, North Dakota

Traveling With Oz
A road lined with beauty can lure many in, sometimes the road is leading to evil.
Keep traveling the path and it soon passes the evil and is wickedly beautiful.

Carl Hentsch
Saint Joseph, Missouri

The Clock of the Time Dragon and The City of Emeralds
WICKED - knowing the past, present and future. A clock that doesn't tell time. The stage is set. I am always awed and inspired by the stage, a clock that reveals all secrets. Truly WICKED!

FINALIST

Sylvia Hernandez

Brooklyn, New York

Wicked NYC

I have always had a special place in my heart for the Wicked Witch of Oz, so I had to make this quilt. After lots of research and drawings I went back to something I learned as a child. I wrote and cut out the word WICKED the way we did to make snowflakes. The rest of the quilt just came together as I went along.

FINALIST

Pat Hilderbrand

Columbia, Missouri

Who's Watching

Is the Wicked Witch watching? Or is someone else hiding behind the mask?

The animals know. The Wicked Witch is watching out for them because she is wicked GOOD!

Can you see the elephant, a bird, a fish, and even a flying monkey?

Stephanie Horsley

Los Angeles, California

Di-vine-ly Wicked

In the musical *WICKED*, I love that the premise of the story is things are not as always as they seem. Vines can often be binding, but they can also hold great beauty, and can be beautiful in their own way. This musical has very special personal meaning to me and it was such a pleasure to create this piece in honor of my own best friend and to celebrate the show's tremendous success.

Staci Hurt
Orange, California

Something Wicked This Way Comes

Raven is made from black paper. Cherrywood greens echo the branches that are stenciled on.
There is a clock and gears on the moon as Raven plots his web for the evening's festivities.

Nancy Hutchison
Kennesaw, Georgia

Labyrinth

This quilt represents a life journey through a labyrinth with its own twists, turns, and flying monkeys.
The optical illusion of Oz is created through color and value placement. Be sure to view this quilt from
a distance to see the 3-D effect. But beware of the WICKED flying monkeys!

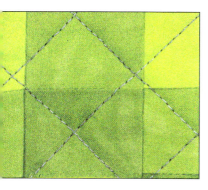

Kara Jamison
Collegedale, Tennessee

The Wicked Tornado

April 27, 2011: tornadoes change the appearance of our neighborhood, and our neighbors' lives in thousands of ways. The first time I saw the challenge fabrics and topic, I knew I had to create a tornado. So I studied photographs, artist's re-creations, and the science of tornadoes. Since the original story of Oz began with a tornado, this is dedicated to Dorothy and Toto and the others who have experienced *The WICKED Tornado*.

Wicked Cool

Tina Johnson

Tina Johnson
Champaign, Illinois

Wicked, Windy and Wild

I always enjoyed art and found my medium in cloth, needle, and thread. I create by using hand piecing and quilting as my technique because I enjoy the textile experience. I am interested in antique quilts and methods, but like taking that knowledge to create a piece of art that is current and forward thinking. I was recently inspired by a meeting with the ladies of Gees Bend. I thought this project would best be represented by using a variation of their methods. This allowed not only the gradual development of this piece, but also the free-form expression of WICKED.

Elaine Jones
Omaha, Nebraska

Wicked Jacamar Eye

My sewing began with 4-H and high school home economics. Sewing expanded to family and home and, seven years ago, a decision to saturate my family with quilts. Into 2010, I fledged to fiber arts with subject matter heavily influenced by graphic art and my love of nature. I live in West Omaha with Lucy and Desi, two helpful kitties, and have expanded saturation to include not just family, but also friends and my own home with both quilts and fiber art.

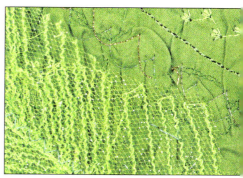

FINALIST

Anita Karban-Neef

Cary, Illinois

Wicked…Walking!

Nothing makes me feel more powerful, sexy and WICKED like a pair
of statement knee-high boots. Just watch me walking in them.
WICKED… Walking!

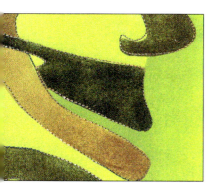

Nancy Kazlaukas
Sauk Centre, Minnesota

Witch Way

We all have good and bad in us that confronts us at different times and in different situations. Much like the branches of a tree, our lives intertwine and create who we are. In the little puzzle of the quilt, you can find a witch's hat, high-heeled shoe, star, moon, spider and spiderweb. Each day we face the question: "Which way ... will we be good or bad, noble or wicked, honorable or evil... *Witch Way* will we go today?"

FINALIST

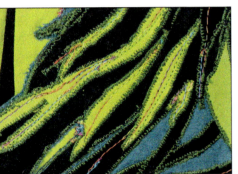

Deanna Keller

Indian Trail, North Carolina

Greener Pastures

This is an autobiographical journey, dedicated to my sweet daughter Hannah: a future Elphaba. It's my statement about leaving the "popular" Glinda mold of all I've previously been told that a wife/woman should be. I was forced to accept, reminding myself who I was prior to an abusive relationship: smart, competent, and a good kind of different. But I want to be comfortable in my green skin. So, let green be the new black! I'm defying gravity … to greener pastures, to a new me: unlimited. Freedom is bringing a bright future for us both, I know. It's just a matter of time.

Robin Kingsbury
Brooklyn, New York

A Wicked Wind on the Horizon

As a New Yorker I have fortunately seen *WICKED* numerous times, dating all the way back to the original cast. Although the book and the musical take place before Dorothy, I couldn't get the image of the threatening twister out of my mind. Upon receipt of the beautiful Cherrywood Fabrics, I decided to create the menacing whirlwind and wickedness of a tornado. The greens reminded me of the sky color when a tornado is on the way. I used appliqué and free motion quilting, intentionally using dark thread on the back to mimic my initial line drawing for the design.

FINALIST

Lisa Koehler
Reddick, Illinois

I'm Not That Girl

When I came upon the ad for the WICKED Cherrywood Challenge, I knew I had to do it.
I was excited at the possibility of representing Cherrywood Fabric and being able to create the
celebration of *WICKED's* 11th anniversary. I wanted her eyes to be telling you a story, her story.
The frayed edges of the fabric were intentional to show a little more realistic view - that her
story of life is frayed and vulnerable. And the way her hair is blowing in the wind defies gravity.
The keyboard represents the musical.

Robin Koenig
Saratoga, California

Wicked
I loved the musical so it was super fun to participate especially
with the delicious fabrics from Cherrywood!

Sarah Lanese

Hixson, Tennessee

Winged Wickedness
Being fascinated by both Cherrywood Fabric and the musical *WICKED*,
I couldn't let this challenge "pass me by."

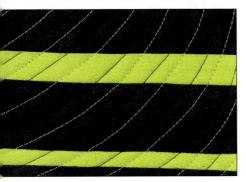

FINALIST

Nancy LaPorte

Prattville, Alabama

Surrender Dorothy

My mom wouldn't let me watch The Wizard of Oz because it always scared me. I'd beg. She'd relent. Then I begged to leave the bedroom lights on! This quilt is of one of my favorite scenes in the movie. I wanted to frame the picture so it looked like the photo. The clock face from the play encompasses the scene from the movie. Whether it's "There's no place like home" or "Are we born WICKED or have wickedness thrust upon us?" the message is universal and touches us.

Kitty Lewis
Shadyside, Ohio

Elphaba = Idina Menzel

This is a pictorial quilt of Idina Menzel. I used a technique I learned at a class in Columbus, OH, "Making Faces" taught by Maria Elkins. The face was made separate and then appliquéd on the background. I also used trapunto quilting for her hat and body, raw edge appliqué and hot fixed crystals. All fabrics are Cherrywood. I have also loved *WICKED* and so excited to do this challenge.

Kathy Lincoln
Burke, Virginia

Wicked Cool!

This quilt was a challenge in more than one sense of the word. I had a plan early in the process but had to wait until I had enough time to execute the plan. Finally on July 21, I had the time. The original plan just wouldn't come together, no matter what I did. So I threw out that plan and started over. "WICKED!" was something that my late sister-in-law Nancy said all the time. So I started with "wicked cool" and progressed from there. It wasn't until I had the whole plan and things started that I realized that July 21 was the first anniversary of Nancy's death. So this quilt is dedicated to her.

Sandy Lindfors

Live Oak, Florida

Wicked - You Betcha!

The challenge came to my attention with a swift poke from "Florence" (my inner muse). "Lookie here girlie, you can do this!" A chartreuse green informational flyer in hand, she pushed and gnawed at my creative spot until she had my attention. "What could be better?" she said. "We both love all things Oz and WICKED and to do it with Cherrywood Fabrics … it's a wrap!" Having grown up in Duluth and majored in art at UMD in the 60's only made it sweeter. I love challenges and Cherrywood. WICKED? Yes I am! *You Betcha!*

Vickie Lord
Atlanta, Georgia

Spiraling Into Wickedness

Nobody is born WICKED. It's more of a slow spiral down. We start out innocent and happy. Then comes that one bad decision, that WICKED deed. We make justifications, but the next act is so much easier. Before we know it, we're on a downhill spin and spiraling into wickedness. The colors move from bright and happy lime green and hot pink into progressively darker and more pensive greens, ending finally with black.

Julie Luoma
Auburn, Washington

Time To Be Wicked

WICKED can be evil, mean-spirited, clever, bad to the bone, razor-sharp humorous. Intriguing with an element of fear. A clock with evil eyes behind it, a beautiful but deadly dragon. Impressively sharp points that can pierce anything. Graceful curves to draw you closer. It's all here. Beautiful but slightly discordant. I've used Angle Play templates for the piecing, machine embroidery for the dragon and clock face, real clock hands and free motion embroidery.

Linda Maether
Shipshewana, Indiana

Something Wicked This Way Comes
Pieced four-block quilt with machine embroidery designs used with permission by Urban Threads.
Machine quilted and bound.

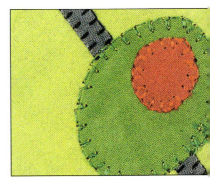

Zeeda Magnuson
Minneapolis, Minnesota

Wickedly Good Beverages: Well, we can't all come and go by bubble!
The dichotomy & thought process: Elphie/Glinda, wicked/good, dry personality/bubbly personality, martini/champagne, Glinda travels by wand and bubble/Elphie travels by broom. I portrayed the personalities of the leads of *WICKED* with two beverages. Elphie is characterized by the martini glass' sturdy and strong base, with a broom swizzle. Glinda's bubbly personality is characterized by the champagne flute with a wand stem. Magic is seen swirling upward, creating the bubbles in which she travels. Who wouldn't be happy traveling on champagne bubbles?

Sally Manke
Arcadia, Michigan

Elphaba & The Time Dragon

My work in fiber art is intended to tell a story, capture a mood or cause the viewer to reflect on a thought. Seeing the show on Broadway surrounded by high school students on spring break inspired me create this quilt. *Elphaba & The Time Dragon* shows the beauty and determination of Elphaba while the threat of the Time Dragon Clock, with all it's secrets, hangs over her. This mixed-media piece shows where real beauty comes from, with the use of artistic expression and precise technical quilting.

FINALIST

Karen Marchetti

Port St. Lucie, Florida

Elphie

What an awesome challenge! I knew immediately I wanted to participate. The colors are amazing, the subject matter is beyond total coolness – although I have yet to see WICKED, I researched everything possible. I knew I wanted a crazy-haired Elphaba, and had to include the clock of the Time Dragon. I also wanted to incorporate some flying monkeys without taking away from Elphie. I drew out the clock and worked Elphie's hat and hair to fill the space. Techniques include raw-edge appliqué, turned-edge appliqué, trapunto, machine quilted on my Gammill.

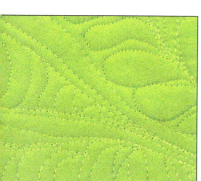

Karen Markely
Trabuco Canyon, California

Elphaba

I love Cherrywood Fabrics and the challenge to use nothing else was intriguing. I wanted to portray the main character in a recognizable way without it being just a copy of the poster. My free-flowing design worked well with the soft curves of her hat. The quilt is pieced with a netting overlay. Wool batting fills out the open spaces nicely.

Joan Maxwell
Russells Point, Ohio

The Sun Also Shines on the Wicked

Pulling together various iconic images from the Broadway musical *WICKED* and combining them with the original elements and a wickedly wonderful Cherrywood Fabric palette yielded a glimpse into Elphaba's world where *The Sun Also Shines on the Wicked*. Photo transferred images on silk organza, fused challenge fabric combined with fabric paint highlights, and machine quilting capture a moment of time in this daunting and sinister world

M. Leana McCutcheon

Roxbury, New Jersey

Wicked

The sorceress tempts us to believe in her magic ... magic that has kept her on Broadway for 11 years; magic of friendship that last as long as memories exist. Creating art quilts is an essential part of who I am. I am inspired by how light affects color and love to play with fabric. I get excited when challenged to make something new and unique using traditional quilt technique and materials. When each piece comes together, I smile and feel complete.

Jennifer McRae
Cedar Rapids, Iowa

Bubbles Are Overrated

The inspiration for this quilt was "Defy Gravity." I love the way each character does this in her own special way. The techniques used in the making of this quilt were free-standing lace embroidery, quilted appliqué (some with organza overlay), embroidered lettering, and embroidered patches. The Swarovski crystals were added to represent the famous ruby slippers.

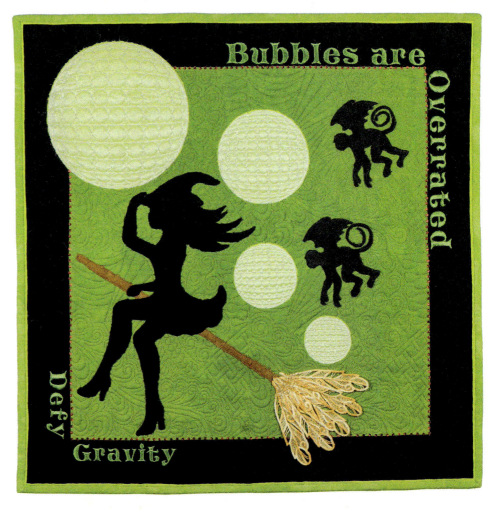

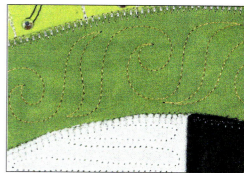

Sandra Messore
Hollis, New Hampshire

Good and Evil
Think positive about your past, present and future. Look through the eyes of the Good Witch.
No matter what you see, throw out the evil and think positive.

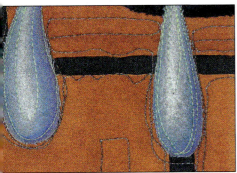

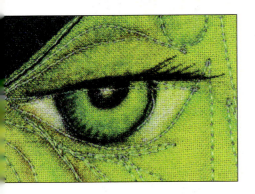

Pam Moller
Beloit, Wisconsin

She's Melting
I must be a bit WICKED … There have been times I wished some people would just melt away. What a fantastic dream to be able to just throw water on someone and they would simply disappear.

LouAnn Moore
Sherman, Illinois

Wicked In Your Mind

Bad WICKED - the root of wicked evil is sometimes controlled by madness or money. All the money in the world may not buy peace of mind and calm emotions. Walking on a dark night, around a corner, there is a glowing creature and blood. The immediate emotion is stop, turn, run. Evil wicked is in front of you. Is it a covered hood or someone's head, a dark creature hunting for food, or a black cat wearing a sparkling red collar? Mean, evil wicked is still something that has to be dealt with by all people.

Carol Morgen
Roberts, Wisconsin

Green Elixir

I believe one of the most wicked acts is to have an extramarital affair, which is what Elphaba's mother did with a traveling salesman. He persuaded her mother to "have a little drink of green elixir." Upon Elphaba's birth, "like a froggy, ferny cabbage, the baby was unnaturally green!" her father rejected her – another WICKED act!

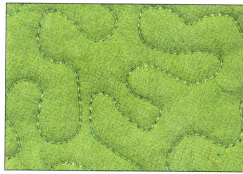

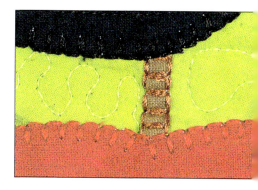

Jane Newman

Ithica, New York

Temptation

Participating in this 2014 Cherrywood Challenge was such fun in that it allowed me to express my wickedly creative (or creatively WICKED) side. I thoroughly enjoyed working with those luscious fabrics and striking colors. The end result is an image I believe everyone can relate to in their own way. The struggle between good and evil is a universal one. The temptation to "be wicked" lies within all of us. What then is the impulse that compels us to "let it out?"

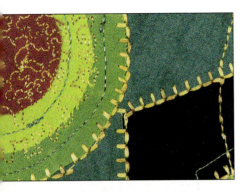

Wendy Nickel

Kiester, Minnesota

Accepting Limits

As a beginning quilter, inspiration was gathered from quilter Susan Cleveland and scenes from the musical *WICKED*. This is a patchwork version of "like a comet pulled from orbit ..."
- Stephen Schwartz, music/lyrics

Charlotte Noll
Lauderhill, Florida

Wicked Wilma Weather

My quilt depicts the *Wicked Wilma Weather* my family experienced in October 2005. I've lived in Florida for over 30 years and each hurricane season we prepare for storms. Thankfully we rarely have more than just normal wet summer weather. But in 2005 Hurricane Wilma hit and when I thought of the word "WICKED" for this challenge, Wilma came to mind. We were very lucky but will always remember wicked Wilma.

Judy O'Connor Chaffee
Naperville, Illinois

Wicked Sorcery

Growing up in Kansas City, I witnessed the devastating F5 tornado in 1957. Living in fear of tornadoes was real to me. As anyone who's taken shelter from a tornado knows, that taste of fear - it never goes away. My dreams included the Wizard of Oz tornado. In reading WICKED, I was fascinated by Elphaba's main use of sorcery: the creation of flying monkeys. In her own words she states: "I have flying monkeys and I'm not afraid to use them." My quilt is a kind of dream world, and answers the question: could Elphaba and her monkeys also create tornadoes?

Gail Oliver
Roswell, Georgia

Awakening Wicked

Elphaba decides to trust her beliefs and not judge right from wrong based on other's values. "Defying Gravity" is her declaration of her path in life. Unfortunately, sometimes Elphaba is WICKED to make her point.

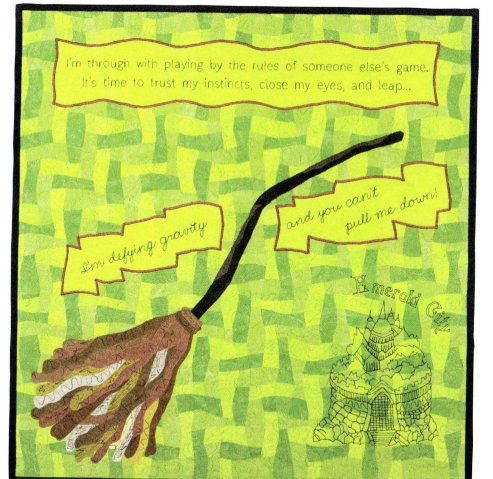

I'm through with playing by the rules of someone else's game. It's time to trust my instincts, close my eyes, and leap...

I'm defying gravity

and you can't pull me down!

Emerald City

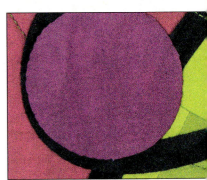

Lynne Ott
Webster City, Iowa

A Victim of Wickedness
The black bubbles and tendrils represent Type 1 diabetes pulling its victim into the black swirl. The pink and purple bubbles are wishing to escape the darkness of this disease.

Susan Pagano
Philadelphia, Pennsylvania

Wicked

I combined my passion for quilting and my favorite hand-dyed fabrics with my favorite Broadway show; what a fun challenge!

FINALIST

FINALIST

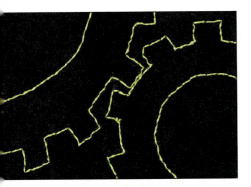

Peg Pennell

Ashland, Nebraska

A Wicked Twister

My *WICKED* inspired piece represents the twists and turns Elphaba's life took as she twirled towards her unwanted wicked future. The tornado as well as the unusual clock from OZ are incorporated into my design. The sprockets so prevalent in the set are integrated into the quilting of the piece. I enjoyed working on this piece inspired by a favorite Broadway show and using the wonderfully sumptuous Cherrywood Hand Dyed Fabrics in one of my favorite colors!

Diane Powers-Harris
Monroe, New Hampshire

Wicked? Influences and Choices

WICKED, a lighthearted musical, details the untold story of the witches of Oz thereby helping us to understand the influences leading these women to make choices that ultimately created such unique personas of storyland. Looking deeper, we find the underlying storyline also deals with political issues, societal mores and the uniqueness of personality. So, we ask, "Was Elphaba, in particular, truly wicked?" Or is she perhaps felt to be such due to a misunderstanding of her choices based on the influences in her life?

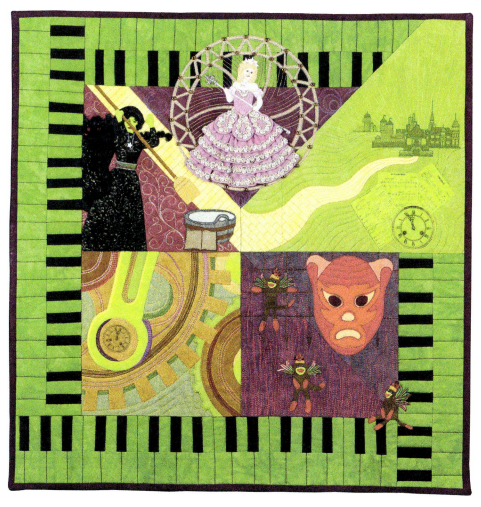

Kim Procknow
Grants Pass, Oregon

Wicked Tongue

My interpretation of the WICKED Challenge came about one evening while listening to my daughter relay an argument she had with her sister in which cruel, unkind words were spoken. That made me think "What can be more wicked than the tongue?" The tongue is sharp and black to represent the WICKED words that come out of a beautiful mouth (full red lips). The teardrops represent the resulting pain.

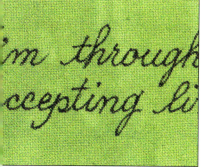

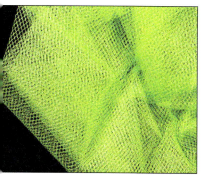

Janet Ratner
Wantagh, New York

Defying Gravity

"*Defying Gravity*"-- my favorite song from *WICKED*, my favorite play! How could I not be inspired to enter The Wicked Cherrywood Challenge? As I have gone skydiving several times, defying gravity has special significance to me.

Shelli Ricci

Apple Valley, Minnesota

Witches' Britches

I wonder ...what hides under the dress of a WICKED girl? *Witches' Britches* is a whimsical look inside the closet and under the dress of one "not-so-nice" girl. For this quilt, I reached inside my bag of tricks and pulled out a pinch of Angelina fiber, a dozen Caran d'Ache crayons, a handful of rubber stamps, a sprinkling of beads and some bling. I think it would be so fun to wear a pretty purple corset and stockings. Maybe good girls have WICKED secrets hiding in their closets too!

Stacye Richardson
Memphis, Tennessee

Wicked … According to Whom?

Like Elphaba, we should all have a climactic moment when we decide to no longer be defined by others but instead we choose to become the person we were created to be. From that moment we are free in ways we cannot imagine, even to the point of Defying Gravity. The second time I saw *WICKED* I was amazed to find myself on the edge of my seat, anxious for Elphaba's powerful voice to remind me to keep defying gravity.

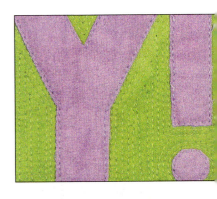

Debbie Rodgers

Suisun City, California

Lemons and Melons and Pears. Oh My!

Oh, the possibilities! When considering all that is WICKED, I mulled over various lyrics, quotes and scenes as I considered the Cherrywood Fabrics. And then I realized it had to be lemons, melons and pears, oh my!

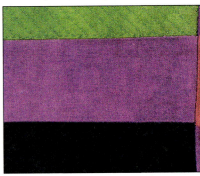

Heather Rose
Livermore, California

The Emerald Thief

The project was well-timed with my re-reading of the original Oz books by Baum. In my travels I have re-met several favorite characters and been reminded of how many strange folk inhabit the land of Oz. The country is mostly peaceful & prosperous, but there are WICKED witches and crooked magicians within this fairy realm. I noticed they are always far flung from the society of Emerald City. But amid so many loyal citizens, is it possible to have one bad apple? Maybe not during the day, but at night, who guards the precious emeralds of Ozma's city?

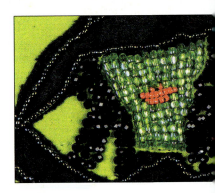

Scarlett Rose

Anderson, California

Defying Gravity

This quilt was made using raw-edge appliqué with hand beading, hand embroidery, hand & machine quilting. I requested an outline drawing from Whitney Kane, my 18-year-old great-niece, which I used as the pattern, adding clothing details and all the embellishments. The image on this quilt represents my strongest and most lasting impression of the musical *WICKED*. I can still see Elphaba rising onstage while singing this song, making this powerful memory the one that I had to attempt for this challenge. This song is one of my all-time musical favorites!

Patti Sandage
Middleton, Tennessee

As Time Runs Out

The quilt is based on my mental image of the guardian dragon of the time clock and Elphaba's sadness at 13 o'clock. This was my first experience using Cherrywood and found it a joy to work with!

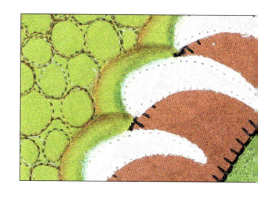

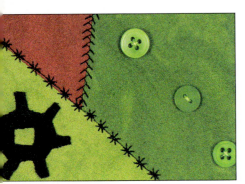

Susan Scheper
Cockeysville, Maryland

Crazy Wicked

I needed inspiration for this challenge. I consider myself more of a traditional quilter but wanna-be Art Quilter. I saw *WICKED* the musical at Gershwin Theater this July and thought it was crazy good. My entry is a traditional crazy quilt with a WICKED modern theme.

Debby Schindall
DelRay Beach, Florida

Wicked Black Cats

This quilt is my interpretation of a WICKED black cat. My black cat Tubby loves to be outside stalking through the tall grass, keeping all of the birds on alert. The central motif is her wicked face, surrounded by a border of 'hisses'. The hiss is her response to my attempts to bring her indoors. The quilting in the four corners is designed to look like the tall grass. To enhance the look of nature, I sprayed sizing over the quilting to force color variations.

Linda Shafe

Springfield, Michigan

No One Mourns the Wicked

The lyrics and quotes from the musical inspired me to create this quilt.

Betsy Shannon
Minneapolis, Minnesota

Toto ...Drop It!

These colors are my favorite. I finished the trees and it still needed something. So I added a dog and girl, Toto and Dorothy. They remind me of our new little black puppy who has already ruined three pairs of my shoes. I have a new red pair of shoes that I need to hide!

Debbie Silva
Deatsville, Alabama

She Closed Her Eyes and Leapt...
She closed her eyes and leapt - "Defying Gravity."
The curved flying geese and spinning pinwheel represent Elphie's leap and flight.

Janis Stoker
Grants Pass, Oregon

A Palace of a Different Color
One of the things I remember from the movie *The Wizard of Oz* was when Dorothy, upon seeing a horse constantly changing color, inquired "What kind of a horse is that?" and the Cabby replied "He's The Horse of a Different Color, you've heard tell about." I envisioned the Wicked Witch casting a spell on the palace to create *A Palace of a Different Color*. The small monkeys and metal gears connect the quilt to the theme and sets used in WICKED. By adding the yellowish green road, I was able to connect the worlds of both the movie and the play.

Karin Strom-Shikaloff

Leavensworth, Washington

The Wicked Web She Spins

This was the first time I used Cherrywood Fabrics and I really enjoyed working with them. The design just came to me. I like the subject and the colors appealed to me.

Lynn Sudbeck
Pierre, South Dakota

Second Nature

Nature or nurture as to a person's wickedness is one of the themes of the musical *WICKED*. I think we all have a little (or more?) capacity for wickedness in us as "second nature." I used a "twister" quilt pattern background for the tornado in the original *Wizard of Oz* story, appliquéd Elphaba, bobbin-quilted her hair strands, pieced the border to extend the hat and melted painted metallic Tyvek on the words. I love this musical and have seen it in Chicago and Portland. I loved this challenge and I love Cherrywood Fabrics!

Linda Syverson-Guild

Bethesda, Maryland

Wicked Twist

My quilt adds a *Wicked Twist* to classic tales involving WICKED attitudes. The twister has moved across the Kansas countryside, but it picked up more than Dorothy's house. Drawn into the funnel are Snow White's apple, the Queen of Heart's crown, a spindle from Sleeping Beauty, cherries taken from Rapunzel and Rumpelstiltskin, and a gingerbread man from Hansel and Gretel.

Janis Taylor
Salem, Missouri

Twisted Witch
I have always loved Cherrywood Fabrics. As soon as I walked into the Cherrywood booth at Paducah, I took a bundle of the challenge fabric. By the time I left Paducah, I had a picture of the quilt in my mind but had to figure out how to make it.

Sherry Taylor
Lincoln, Nebraska

It's All About The Shoes

Before this project, I had never designed a quilt before. It's not as easy as it seems. For me, projects are about the process and the accomplishment of the end result. I've always been a huge fan of *The Wizard of Oz* and have coveted those ruby slippers since I was a child. When I saw *WICKED*, I learned those shoes were actually silver. At any rate, life is about the shoes and the powers within.

Jamie TenBrink
Coopersville, Michigan

Wicked Good Fun
I came across the contest online and loved the fabric. I haven't seen the musical but wanted to incorporate part of it into the quilt. Thanks for a great contest!

Jenny Wagner
San Jose, California

Defying Gravity

Memories of seeing *WICKED* in Chicago almost ten years ago, in addition to listening to the amazing soundtrack, provided endless inspiration for this quilt. I decided to feature Elphaba's courage and beauty, and the hidden friendship with Glinda. I adapted the Oz gate to have XI for eleven Broadway seasons of *WICKED*! Can you find my favorite lyric hidden in the quilt? Hand appliquéd, hand embroidered and machine quilted.

Jann Warfield
Sarasota, Florida

Wicked Twister

A tornado can be a thing of beauty and fascination. It can also be destructive and can change lives. It becomes a turning point in the lives of the people it affects. There are stories "before the tornado" and different stories "after the tornado." *Wicked Twister!*

Donna Weber
Mahwah, New Jersey

Wickedly Reversible

My quilts are mainly about the quilting, so when I saw this challenge I knew I wanted to show two different images of the stage through quilting. I chose the clock for half of the quilt because of its quiet, reserved beauty – like Elphaba. The other side of course then had to be Glinda and all of her glitz and glamour. I have loved the show since I saw it in previews in October 2003, and fall more in love with it each and every time I see it. *Wickedly Reversible* is my homage to a wonderful show.

Donna Westercamp

Lombard, Illinois

Wicked Wind

Living in the Midwest, we see a lot of windy storms. This quote reminds me of the cyclone that hit Dorothy's house and landed on the bad witch. The quilt twists into a black hole!

Margaret Williams
Tucker, Georgia

Elphaba's Crown of Thorns
In life, as in *WICKED*, things are not always as they seem.

Cindy Wilson
Elysian, Minnesota

Born Wicked?

This is the line that stands out to me as summing up the entire plot. The message believed is often swayed by the appearance, popularity and outgoingness of the messenger. Public relations can be used for good or evil, and human nature is all too eager to believe the worst. The reality of the situation is not always revealed, for many reasons, and people who are publicly enemies may be working together to manipulate the message for their own reasons.

www.cherrywoodfabrics.com

Cherrywood is cotton quilting fabric that has been hand-dyed to look like suede. Our exclusive gradations are the inspiration for quilters, designers, and wearable artists all around the world. Photos do not do justice to this luscious fabric, but once you see it and feel it, you will understand why Cherrywood has such a dedicated following. We start with high-quality muslin and use procion dyes to mix hundreds of colors. These unique formulas are painstakingly developed by our colorist. A team of experts oversees the day-long process and assembly of the beautiful bundles that have made us famous. We have perfected our exclusive technique to produce a beautiful tone-on-tone texture that reads as a solid, but has depth and variety that can never be replicated by mass-production. Cherrywood is proudly made in the U.S.A. by women who sew, create, and dye a little every day.

CHERRYWOOD HAND DYED FABRICS

HOME   100% cotton that looks like suede

The Traveling Exhibit

at the time of this printing

The Gershwin Theater - New York City, New York

The Cherrywood Store/Colorz Quilt Shop - Brainerd, Minnesota

Road to California Quilt Show - Ontario, California

Embroiderer's Guild of America National Exhibition - Morris, Minnesota

AQS QuiltWeek® - Lancaster, Pennsylvania

International Quilt Festival - Chicago, Illinois

The Arts Center In Orange - Orange, Virginia

AQS QuiltWeek® - Paducah, Kentucky

Minnesota Quilt Show - Duluth, Minnesota

AQS QuiltWeek® - Syracuse, New York

AQS QuiltWeek® - Grand Rapids, Michigan

AQS QuiltWeek® - Chattanooga, Tennessee

AQS QuiltWeek® - Des Moines, Iowa

Pacific International Quilt Festival - Santa Clara, California

Thank you!

I would like to thank all who participated in our first official challenge of this scale. Whether you finished your quilt, bought the fabric bundle with good intentions, or simply fanned the flames with your enthusiasm, your support was much appreciated. Cherrywood customers are the best people in the world! The following people stand out on this wicked path. Thank you to the board members of the Quilt Alliance, including Marie Bostwick, Amy Milne and Meg Cox. Their support, enthusiasm, and connections are really what made this idea blossom. Michael Michalski, Dresser in the costume department at WICKED, was a great liason/spokesman for this project. Thank you for the great backstage tour! Susan Sampliner, Company Manager of WICKED, always found time to hear my ideas, answer my questions, and brought this challenge to a higher level. I am so fortunate to have amazing employees who put in countless hours to keep this project organized; Dorothy Cronin hung the entire show at the gallery in one day, and Melissa Yeager coordinated all the traveling exhibit logistics. Carolyn Abbott, Kevin Yeager, Arlene Fitzpatrick, Dorothy Cronin, and Dawn Marks had the impossible task of selecting winners. Maddie Kertay hosted the first traveling display. Cyndi Souder provided invaluable advice and experience. Brenda Lyseng and Trisha Frankland were my book editors. A special thank you goes to my husband, John. His constant encouragement, creative eye, excellent advice, and unending patience kept me sane through a pretty steep learning curve. And last but not least, I need to thank my kids, Isaac, Elsa, and Abram, for tolerating my crazy obsession and the piles of quilts that took over the house for several months.
You are all WICKED awesome!

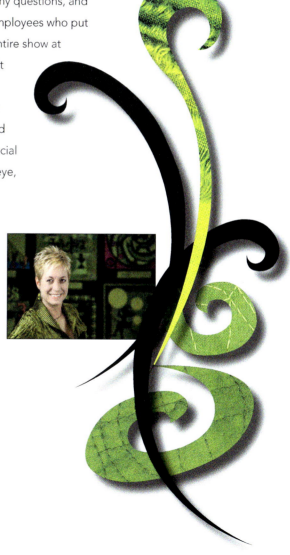

- Karla Overland
  Cherrywood Fabrics